Blog Your Book into Existence

Richter Publishing

Write & Publish a Book Series

By Tara Richter

Edited by Casey Cavanagh

& Alex Gonzalez

ISBN: 0692275908
ISBN-13: 9780692275900

DISCLAIMER

FOREWORD

"I was so excited to be one of Tara's clients to be coached through the writing and publishing process! I have never written a book, so I knew when I wanted to embark on this journey; she was the one I needed to contact. Since she already had three books under her belt, I called her to find out how she did it. I was amazed after our phone conversation that she had discovered a quick and easy way to get a book published in only a few months. I didn't even think that was possible! I knew Kevin and I had to work with her on our project. I really wanted our book to come from the heart and soul so it would resonate with the reader. It was a challenging journey, but Tara's tips and coaching has really made the process a breeze. She's helped us every step of the way and looked out for me, Tara keeps me on track with my goal. If I can write and publish a book with no experience, you can too!"

- Anthony Amos Multi Founding franchisor & partnership expert

http://theanthonyamos.com/

"When Anthony and I decided to publish a joint book, he said he wanted it to be available for sale within a few months. I thought he was crazy, we wouldn't have enough time in our hectic schedules to get this done. However, when we brought Tara aboard, her coaching techniques made it easy. She has streamlined the writing and publishing process, utilizing every spare minute for maximum results. Even with my super busy schedule I can get a book done. She utilizes every spare second you have. If you want to be a published author, Tara is the one to get the job done!"

- Kevin Harrington, Shark from ABC's "Shark Tank"

http://kevinharrington.tv/

CONTENTS

INTRODUCTION

A blog is the easiest and quickest way to drive traffic to your website, your company, and your products. It gets you ranked high in Google if done properly and is also a functional way to write your book. I will walk you through the steps of how to: start a blog, use keywords for SEO, organize your blogs for your book, and get 4,000 organic hits a month. (Organic means free, in case you were thinking of non-hormone injected chicken breasts.)

We will setup the blog through WordPress and utilize their features. There are other blogging sites out there, but I have had greater results with WordPress. If you already have a blog set-up through a different site, you can still utilize the SEO (Search Engine Optimization) features within here. However, the step-by-step instructions will be on a WordPress platform. You can always set up a new blog through them because it is free.

The examples that I am going to show you here in this guide is from my blog for my book series, "The Dating Jungle." I started this blog about 3 years ago after publishing my first book, "10 Rules to Survive the Dating Jungle." I now have 6 books in the series; 3 first editions and 3 second editions. I wrote my second book, "10 Rules to Survive the Internet Dating Jungle" all through blogging. These are all my tips and tricks I discovered along the way.

Are you ready to enter the beautiful world of blogging?! Get ready to roll up your sleeves and have some fun!

Sincerely,

Tara Richter

CHAPTER 1 HOW TO START A BLOG

Follow these easy step-by-step instructions to set up your blog if you do not currently have one.

1) Go to www.wordpress.com

2) Click "Get Started" button

3) Enter your email address, username and password (the password needs to be complex otherwise it won't accept it ex: Tr337513&)

4) Now choose your blog address. This part is important. You need to choose something that involves the keywords that other people used while searching for you in Google. This part is going to get a little technical.

What is a Keyword and Why Should I Care? Search engines (Google, Bing, etc.) scan your website on a daily/hourly basis for new content. They then index that content so that others, using the same search engine, can find it easily when they search for the kind of content you have. SEO is the process of writing that content on your page to help tell the search engines how they should index your site. The keywords on your site, blog, and social media pages are the words or phrases that someone types into a search engines to find your website. An example of keywords for coffee shop would be: *coffee, coffee beans, fresh roasted coffee, who has the best coffee, where can I get a latte in downtown Clearwater, etc.*

    a.   So now that we know what keywords and SEO is, you need to have this in the URL of your blog. **What is a URL?** Universal Resource Locator Ex:

http://tampadatingjungle.wordpress.com/

        i.   For my dating blog site, I chose "Tampa Dating Jungle" for my blog address. It has keywords that people would search for dating in the Tampa area. Pick something short and sweet but relevant to your business.

    b.   Search keywords to find out what people are searching for in the product, service, or whatever topic you are writing your book about. It's as easy as going into Google's search engine and typing something you find relevant. For my coaching business and my first three books, it's *Dating Advice, Dating Coach, Dating Coach Tampa.* Start entering a word and let Google auto populate the rest. I discovered lots of people were searching "10 Rules of Dating." I never even knew that until Google told me. Now it's one of my key search terms.

What are your key search terms? Write them down here:

_____

_____

_____

_____

_____

_____

_____

_____

_____

5) Then click on the left button at the bottom "Create Blog" for the free version. If you wish to upgrade later you can. In order to have the free blog it will display random Ads at the bottom of your blogs. If you pay, it removes those ads.

6) It will send you a confirmation email that you need to check and click on in order to activate the blog.

7) When you click on the emailed link it takes you back to WordPress to set up your blog, fill out the title of your blog, etc. Then hit NEXT STEP

8) **Choose a theme.** WordPress has many free templates you can use.

9) Connect your Twitter and Facebook accounts if you have them, then click NEXT

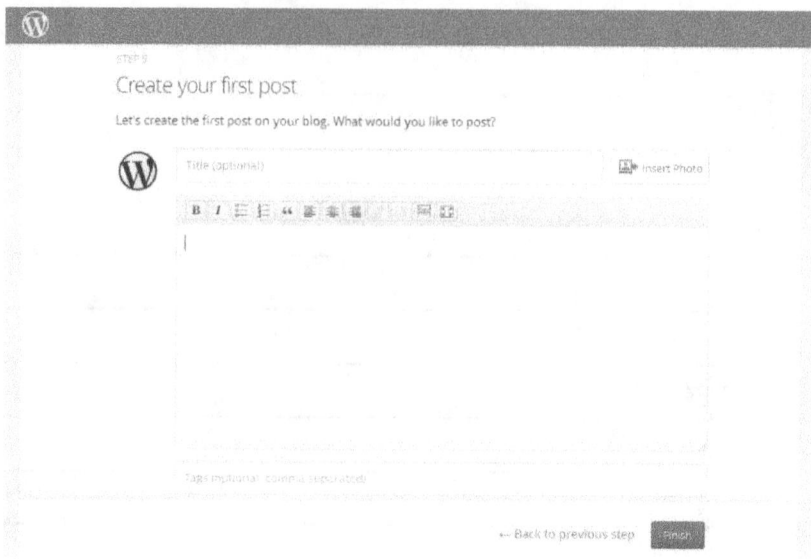

10) Create Your First Post: Select Text

    a. **Title:** Write something that includes key words ex: "10 Ways to Date Safe Online"

    b. **In the body:** Sprinkle your keywords all throughout here. However, don't just list them one by one. Incorporate them in the sentences and thoughts.

    c. **Tags:** Tags is another term for keywords. You will see this used all throughout the internet. They mean the exact same thing. Now this is the spot where you can list all your key terms. I have about fifty or so, too many to remember all the time. So I keep them on a notepad file on my computers desktop, then I can just copy and paste them into this field. Make sure each phrase is separated by a comma. Ex: Dating Jungle, Dating, Dating Advice. Otherwise it will clump them into one phrase.

d. **Upload a photo:** You always want to add photos your posts and videos. It is better for SEO, and it makes your writing more engaging. However, pay attention to what you name your images. Google Image Spiders (internet spiders, not real spiders!) will read the name of the picture in order to determine what it is and what it is relevant to. Ex: I would name my photos: TaraRichterDatingCoach.jpg. Do this prior to uploading it into WordPress.

    i. **What is an internet spider?** Search engines on the Internet use search spiders to index web pages: programs that read through web pages, analyze and assess the content, and enter it in a database.

e. **Publish:** Once you're done, click the blue Publish button and your blog is now available for the world to read!

11) **Fill out the About Section.** You need all your information in "About" for SEO purposes and so readers can contact you or find your business if they like what you have to say. In order to fill that out, go to:

a. **Dashboard:** on the left hand side to find – Users – My Profile – and select it

b. Fill in your bio on the next screen: remember to use your keyword within this section too.

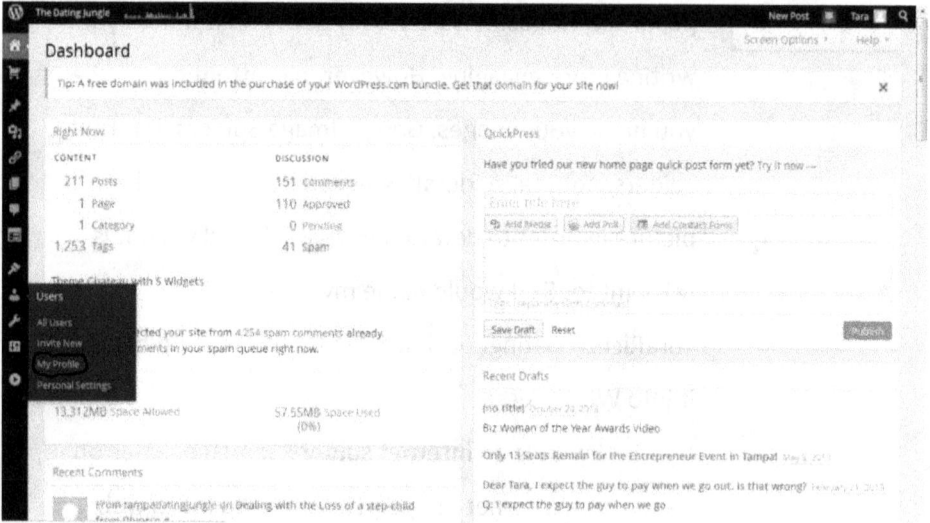

CHAPTER 2 ORGANIZE YOUR BLOG INTO A BOOK

Now that you have your blog set up and ready to go, start organizing your words. If you're not good at just sitting down and writing 10,000 words, blogs can greatly help you write your book. They are much easier because they're done in short chunks. A blog should not be more than 2-3 paragraphs, about 750 words—short, nice, sweet bits of information for the reader. If you publish small bits of information once or twice a week, it gives your audience little teasers of what's to come in your book, building the momentum to purchase it once it's fresh off the press. It gets people excited and gives them a chance to interact with you. They may even give you more ideas to write about! But don't give it all away for free, just bits n' pieces. Follow these steps to assist your blogging in the process of completing your book:

1) Have an outline of your book and how many chapters it has. On your computer, create a folder with the title of your book on it. *Download outline here: http://richterpublishing.com/resources/*

2) Within that folder, create subfolders, one for each chapter.

3) When you write a blog, copy and paste it into a Word document. Name the file the title of the article.

4) Place that Word file in the folder of the appropriate chapter.

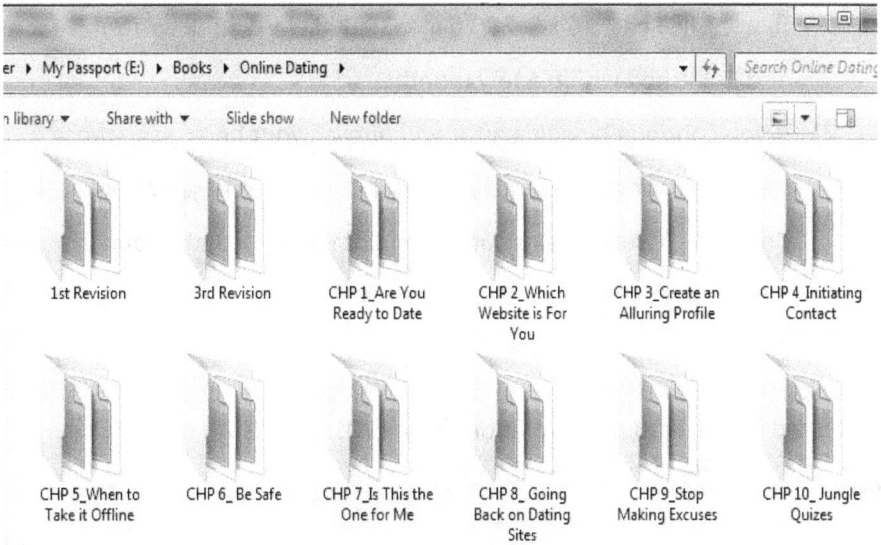

5) **An industry standard 5x8, 100 page book is approximately 20,000 words.** If you blog 4 times a week at 750 words per post, your manuscript would be complete in 8 weeks:

$$750\text{words} \times 4\text{posts} = 3000\text{words}$$

$$\times \ 8\text{weeks} = 2,400\text{words}$$

6) Once you're blogging is complete, take all your Word documents and merge them into one file. Print it out, read it over, and fill in the gaps between the Posts to make the story flow smoothly. I utilized this method with my second book, "10 Rules to Survive the Internet Dating Jungle," and it worked flawlessly. I had a 6 x 9, 200 page, 30,000 word book written and published within a few months.

7) If you continue blogging after you publish your book, save those new posts for publishing the 2nd and 3rd editions of your book. Copy and paste the blogs at the end of the book and re-publish it with fifty extra pages of content!

I released the 1st edition on Valentine's Day 2013 & the 2nd edition August 2013

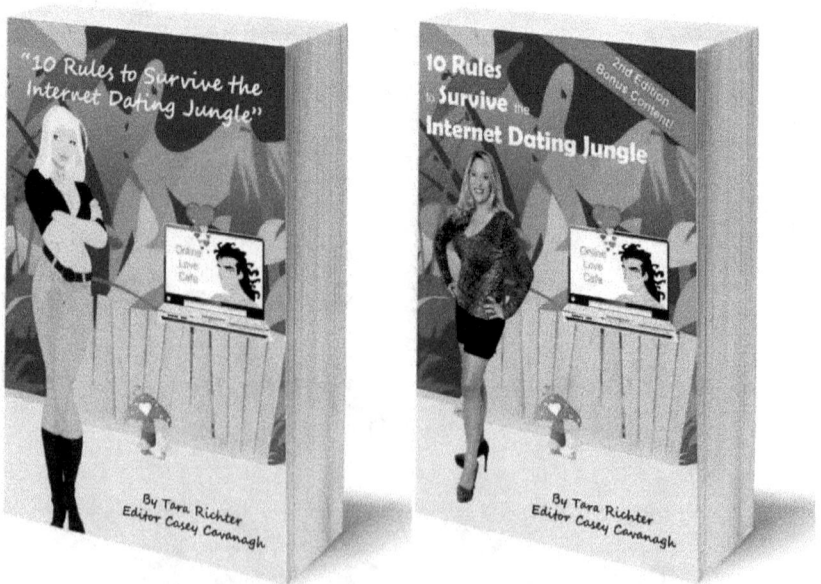

OUTLINE

You can download the book outline from the link I gave earlier in this chapter, or utilize it here to flesh out your book content. Breaking down the subject matter of the books into multiple chapters & sub-chapters will help you when coming up with blog content. It also lets you know what information comes at what point in the book, so it flows in the traditional book format. Remember this is only for cliff notes.

Title Page- includes Title, authors & editors

Dedication - Who do you want to dedicate your book to friends/family?

_____

_____

_____

_____

_____

_____

Table of Contents – This part will be created during formatting process in another course.

Foreword – Usually written by someone with more experience in your industry than yourself _____

_____

_____

Acknowledgements – Who would you like to give credit to for helping the book become a reality? Ex: Mentors, Graphic Designers, Ghost Writers, etc. _____

_____

_____

_____

Introduction – Short synopsis of what the entire book is about. Only needs to be a few pages long. _____

_____

_____

_____

_____

_____

_____

Chapter 1 –Subject:_____

_____

_____

Chapter 1 – Subchapter _____

_____

_____

Chapter 1 – Subchapter_____

_____

_____

Chapter 1 – Subchapter_____

_____

_____

Chapter 2 –Subject:_____

_____

_____

Chapter 2 – Subchapter _____

_____

_____

Chapter 2 – Subchapter_____

_____

_____

Chapter 2 – Subchapter_____

_____

_____

Chapter 3 –Subject:_____

_____

_____

Chapter 3 – Subchapter _____

_____

_____

Chapter 3 – Subchapter_____

_____

_____

Chapter 3 – Subchapter_____

_____

_____

Chapter 4 –Subject:_____

_____

_____

Chapter 4 – Subchapter _____

_____

_____

Chapter 4 – Subchapter_____

_____

_____

Chapter 4 – Subchapter_____

_____

_____

Chapter 5 –Subject:_____

_____

_____

Chapter 5 – Subchapter _____

_____

Chapter 5 – Subchapter_____

Chapter 5 – Subchapter_____

Chapter 6 –Subject:_____

Chapter 6 – Subchapter _____

Chapter 6– Subchapter_____

Chapter 6 – Subchapter_____

Chapter 7 –Subject:_____

Chapter 7 – Subchapter _____

Chapter 7 – Subchapter_____

_____

_____

Chapter 7 – Subchapter_____

_____

_____

Chapter 8 –Subject:_____

_____

_____

Chapter 8 – Subchapter _____

_____

_____

Chapter 8 – Subchapter_____

_____

_____

Chapter 8 – Subchapter_____

_____

_____

Chapter 9 –Subject:_____

_____

_____

Chapter 9 – Subchapter _____

_____

_____

Chapter 9– Subchapter_____

_____

_____

Chapter 9 – Subchapter_____

_____

_____

Chapter 10 –Subject:_____

_____

_____

Chapter 10 – Subchapter _____

_____

_____

Chapter 10 – Subchapter_____

_____

_____

Chapter 10 – Subchapter_____

_____

_____

Final Thoughts/ Summary – A few pages to tie it all up:_____

_____

_____

_____

_____

_____

Author Bio & Photo – Use professional pictures. Keep short and put links to businesses, other books etc. _____

_____

_____

_____

_____

_____

_____

_____

_____

_____

_____

_____

_____

_____

_____

_____

_____

_____

_____

_____

_____

_____

CHAPTER 3 PUBLICIZE/ SHARE YOUR BLOG

When you start posting, you want to turn the Publicize/ Sharing feature on in WordPress. This will sync all your social media sites like, Facebook, Twitter, Pinterest, etc., to your account. When this is hooked up, WordPress blasts your post to all your accounts right when you hit the Publish button. It's very helpful and saves a lot of time. To do this, follow these steps:

1) Log into your WordPress account
2) Click on "My Sites" across the top bar
3) Select "Sharing" under the title of your site

*Note WordPress website has been updated. You can still use "Classic Mode" where the call it Publicize still. Or the new update version calls it "Sharing." We are going to show you the new way which "Sharing."

4) On the right hand side, click SHARING (if it doesn't auto pop up)
5) It will open a box that will show all the Social Media Options
6) Click CONNECT BUTTONS next to the sites that you want to link

7) This should pop up an box to allow you to connect to your Facebook, Twitter, etc.

8) Add as many accounts as you like. The more places you blast out your blog post the more search-ability they will have.

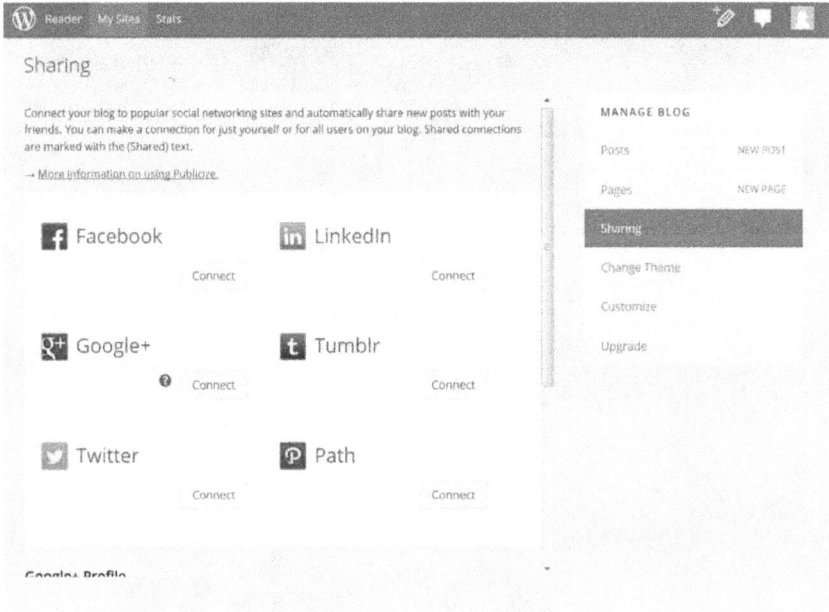

CHAPTER 4 CHECK YOUR STATS WEEKLY

I actually check my stats daily on my popular blogs. I find it exciting to see how many hits a day I get, what part of the country they are coming from and which blogs are receiving the most amount of traffic. Creating a global presence is so easy with a blog. My dating site receives hits from countries I never knew existed! (As demonstrated in a screen shot from my blog on the next page.)

You can learn a lot from your blog's stats. If you are just starting out, it will take a while to see results, but don't get frustrated. The examples I'm going to show you are from blogging for a few years. It does take time, but persistence is key here.

I currently do not blog for The Dating Jungle anymore since I have opened up my publishing company beginning of 2014. The great thing is because I put so much time and effort into the dating blog, it has taken on a life of its own. I don't really have to do anything and I still receive daily hits on my blog.

Awesome example of the power of blogging: I posted an interview I did with actor Ethan Embry on my blog back in Nov 2013. Wikipedia has now linked to my blog as a point of reference for his entry. I'm right in-between People Magazine & TMZ! That's the power of blogging and using the correct key terms for search engines.

http://en.m.wikipedia.org/wiki/Ethan_Embry

/Ethan_Embry

2013	Once Upon a Time	Greg Mendell
2013	Cheap Thrills	Vince
2013	In Security	Kevin
2014	Late Phases	Will

∧ References

1. Ethan Embry - Biography ⏎
2. Ethan Embry Biography (1978-) ⏎
3. "Ethan Embry" ⏎. people.com. 31 March 2003. Retrieved 29 May 2014.
4. http://www.people.com/people/mobile/article/0,,20614981,00.html ⏎
5. "'Can't Hardly Wait' Star Getting Divorced" ⏎. tmz.com. 24 July 2012. Retrieved 29
6. Richter, Tara (30 November 2013). "Tara Richter Interviews Ethan Embry on Datinç tampadatingjungle.wordpress.com. Retrieved 29 May 2014.
7. "Ethan Embry Held Up & Fires Back?" ⏎. tmz.com. 29 November 2006. Retrieved ?
8. "Ethan Embry to Marred Model -- Deal!" ⏎. tmz.com. 19 March 2008. Retrieved 29

∧ External links

- Ethan Embry ⏎ on Twitter
- Ethan Embry ⏎ at the Internet Movie Database
- Ethan Embry ⏎ at AllMovie

Blog Your Book into Existence

Country	Views
United States	35,666
Canada	3,404
United Kingdom	2,947
Australia	1,344
Germany	494
India	334
Philippines	306
South Africa	286
Singapore	256
France	227
Ireland	218
New Zealand	180
Brazil	146
Netherlands	136
Sweden	133
Malaysia	122
Norway	98
Denmark	88
Mexico	83
Belgium	82
Indonesia	78
Italy	76
United Arab Emirates	75
Spain	74
Turkey	68
Poland	60
Israel	58
Thailand	56
Hong Kong	55
Pakistan	53
Japan	47
Switzerland	46
Austria	44
Romania	42
Hungary	42
Croatia	36
Republic of Korea	35
Bulgaria	33
Russian Federation	33
Portugal	32
Kenya	32
Ukraine	32
Taiwan	32
Finland	31
Chile	29
Nigeria	28
Lebanon	27
Argentina	26
Senegal	26
Greece	26
Czech Republic	23
Saudi Arabia	23
Venezuela	23
Egypt	23
Colombia	21
Peru	19
Puerto Rico	18
Latvia	18
Qatar	17
Lithuania	17
Serbia	15
Costa Rica	15
Trinidad and Tobago	14
Slovenia	13
Estonia	13
Kuwait	13
Jamaica	11
Viet Nam	10
Slovakia	10
Grenada	10
Bangladesh	10
Sri Lanka	9

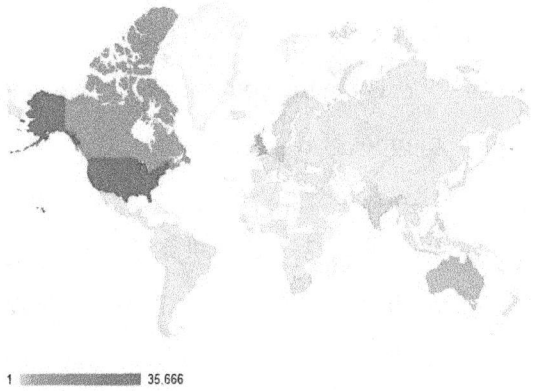

1   35,666

Let's show you where you can find your stats:

1) Log into your WordPress account

2) Click "Stats" across the top of the screen

3) Across the top you will have a blue bar graph showing the number of visits. They parse this out by how many people visited and how many posts they read.

4) Below are your overall stats and, as you see in my example, on my best day I received 334 views. Not too shabby for doing it all for free. I have never run a PPC (pay per click) campaign for this company.

An important thing to monitor is the "Search Engine Terms." We have defined keywords in the beginning of this book. Those are the terms that *you* put for people to find your blog and websites. This WordPress box will tell you the search terms *other people* are typing into Google or Yahoo that brings them to your blog. This is very valuable information. You want to be inside the brains of the people searching for your valuable insights. Some of the words people Googled to find my dating advice blog on that particular day were:

1) how does tinder work
2) over functioning in relationships
3) 3 months dating rule
4) Tampa dating coach
5) zombie wedding dresses

When you start compiling this information, add the appropriate key words into your master list and incorporate them into your SEO efforts. Sometimes people will search strange terms and it will somehow hit your blog. This can inspire you to write new blogs based on that content. I will share with you an example in the next section.

CHAPTER 5 HOW TO RECEIVE 4,000 ORGANIC HITS A MONTH

Again, we're not talking about beating up non-hormone injected chickens here. **Hits** are every time someone looks at your blog. You want as many hits as you can get for free. Blogging is the best way to raise your profile and search ability in Google without paying for it. Whatever topics you are discussing should be interesting enough to drive lots of traffic to your blog once it's up and running. However, some topics may be rather boring. The easiest way to gain traffic is to write about trending topics that are related to your information. For example my Dating Jungle books are about dating and relationships. I watch the popular ABC shows; *The Bachelor, The Bachelorette,* and *The Bachelor Pad* on Monday nights. I write a blog review during the show and post it once the show is done. If you're writing about shows it's important to post ASAP because people are often searching information about the show while it airs.

You want to weave your information within the blog so it's not just about the show. You're getting traffic from people interested in the topic, so they are likely to be interested in your related books. For instance, I will give dating advice like, "He should have said this or that on the date." Then at the bottom I put my information, links to my websites, where to purchase my books, and so forth. Then they stay on my site and read the other blogs as well.

Let's go back to what I was saying earlier, about keeping track of the "Search Engine Terms" people use to find you on Google. During a Bachelor Pad season, I noticed people kept searching the term "Jaclyn Swartz nose job." Swartz is a character within these Bachelor shows. She had a crooked nose in one season, followed by an improved nose on the next one. People wanted to know if she had a nose job. I chose to compose a blog entirely about that subject since it is the number one ranked search term driving people to my site. I researched all over the internet, but I could not find any information confirming whether or not she got a nose job. I concluded from my Photoshop skills that she had not. Low and behold, six months later someone who went to school with her commented on my blog that she did in fact get a nose job!

Weave trending topics throughout your information; comment on situations; offer advice and/or solutions that are relevant to what you're doing. It's all about driving traffic to your site and making people aware of you and your products. When you do blog about those hot topics, remember to put those names, TV shows, etc., in the tag section of that particular blog.

« Return to Stats

Search Terms for all days ending 2013-10-25 (Summarized)

7 Days | 30 Days | Quarter | Year | All time

All Time

Search	Views
jaclyn swartz nose job	305
vanilla sky	166
jaclyn bachelor pad nose job	120
alpha male and alpha female relationship	61
match stir events review	61
alpha male and alpha female	60
desiree hartsock	59
how not to emasculate your man	58
tierra licausi	52
tierra bachelor	48
match stir events	44
overfunctioning	44
selma alameri height	43
stir events	40
how to stop overfunctioning in a relationship	37
overfunctioning women	37
overfunctioning in relationships	36
match.com stir events review	30

2

THOUGHTS ON "DID JACLYN SWARTZ FROM THE BACHELOR PAD GET A NOSE JOB?"

Anonymous person who went to school w her *said:*   April 15, 2013 at 9:35 am

She did.

REPLY
[Edit Comment]

tampadatingjungle *said:*   April 18, 2013 at 5:21 pm

Well there you have it folks, Jaclyn Swartz did in fact have a nose job!

REPLY
[Edit Comment]

LEAVE A REPLY

Enter your comment here

32

CHAPTER 6 PRESELL YOUR BOOK

Now that you have great traffic coming to your blog, capture those readers by pre-selling your book! It's really easy to do. First thing you need to do is open a PayPal account if you do not already have one.

1) Go to www.paypal.com
2) Set up your account information
3) It will take a few days to verify your account if you have never opened one before.

Once that process is done you need to set up a BUY IT NOW button:
1) In your account click on TOOLS across the top
2) Under ACCEPT PAYMENTS ANYWHERE, click PAYPAL BUTTONS
3) Click CREATE BUTTON
4) In the new window that pops up is where you will put all your information for your button.

Create PayPal payment button

PayPal payment buttons are an easy way to accept payments. Check the PayPal Payments Standard Overview for more information. Use this page to customize your button and create the HTML you'll need to copy and paste into your website. Learn more.

Having trouble viewing this page?

▼ Step 1: Choose a button type and enter your payment details

Choose a button type   ⓘ Which button should I choose?
Buy Now ▼

Note: Go to My saved buttons to create a new button similar to an existing one

Item name   Item ID (optional) What's this?
Blog Your Book Into Existence

Price   Currency
10.00   USD ▼   Need multiple prices?

Customize button   Your customer's view

☐ Add drop-down menu with price/option Example
☐ Add drop-down menu Example   **Buy Now**
☐ Add text field Example   VISA

▶ Customize text or appearance (optional)

5) Choose BUY NOW for the button type
6) Put the name of your book in ITEM NAME
7) Set the purchase price

*On a side note, if you are going to be using your button in WordPress, you will need to save the button image from this screen. The reason being is that WordPress uses a link to send someone from your WordPress page to PayPal. Where normally you would copy & paste the html code into a webpage that PayPal provides for the transaction. Put your cursor over the orange button image Right click, that will pull up a menu, then click SAVE IMAGE AS. This will save the image file to your computer to use later.

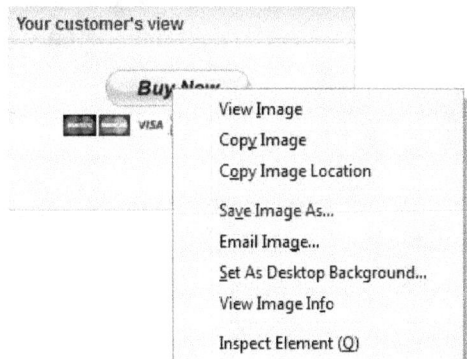

Your customer's view

Buy Now

View Image
Copy Image
Copy Image Location

Save Image As...
Email Image...
Set As Desktop Background...
View Image Info

Inspect Element (Q)

8) Now enter shipping and tax information for your button
9) Click Create Button
10) On the next page is where it's different than most PayPal buttons. Instead of copying the code from the WEBSITE Tab you need to click EMAIL Tab and use that information.

Website	Email

https://www.paypal.com/cgi-bin/webscr?cmd=_s-xclick&hosted_button_id=CVGPKVNCDHY9Y

Select Code   Go back to edit this button

11) Copy this information onto a notepad or Word document and save for later use.

CHAPTER 7 BUY IT NOW BUTTONS IN WORDPRESS

Now we are going to show you how to implement your buttons to make money! You should place a button at the bottom of every blog post you publish. Put pre-sell buttons, then once the book is printed the same button can be used for regular orders. You want to make it as easy as possible for readers to buy your book.

In order to place a button on your page:

1) Open your WordPress account

2) Start a new post or go into an old post

3) Click on the INSERT MEDIA TAB

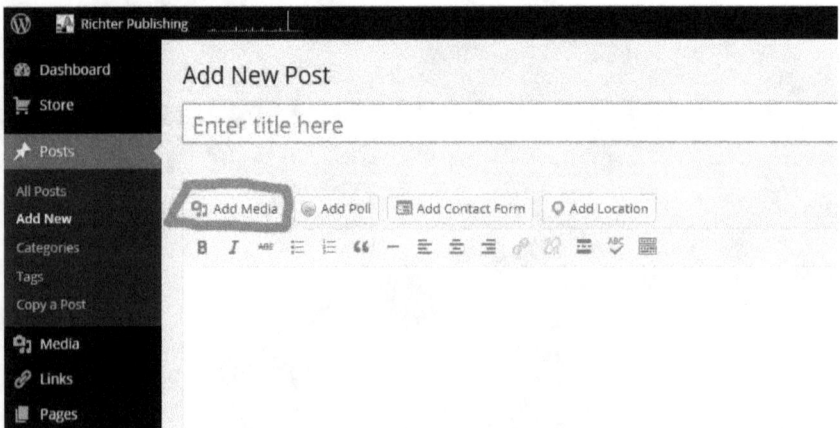

4) On the next screen click UPLOAD FILES tab
5) Then click the button SELECT FILES

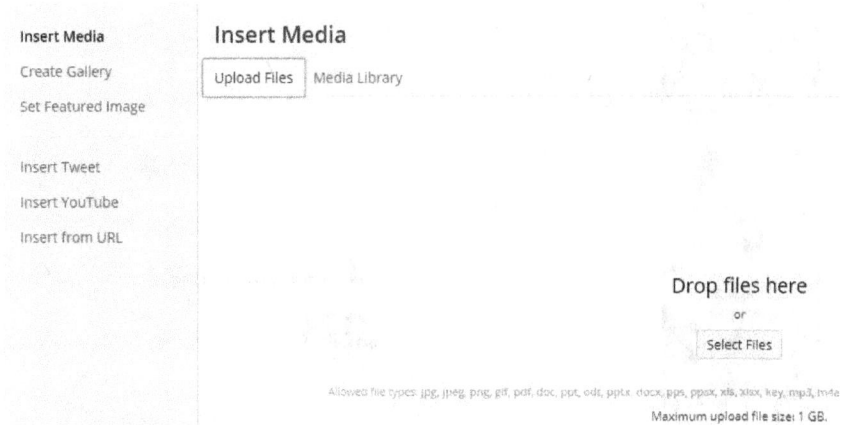

Insert Media	**Insert Media**
Create Gallery	Upload Files Media Library
Set Featured Image	
Insert Tweet	
Insert YouTube	
Insert from URL	

Drop files here

or

Select Files

Allowed file types: jpg, jpeg, png, gif, pdf, doc, ppt, odt, pptx, docx, pps, ppsx, xls, xlsx, key, mp3, m4a

Maximum upload file size: 1 GB.

6) Find the PayPal .JPG image that you saved to your computer from earlier.
7) Once the file is uploaded, click the blue button into the lower right hand corner INSERT INTO POST
8) Now it will go back to the posting screen
9) Here click on the image so a box shows up with handles
10) While you have the image selected, click on the link image across the top of the post.

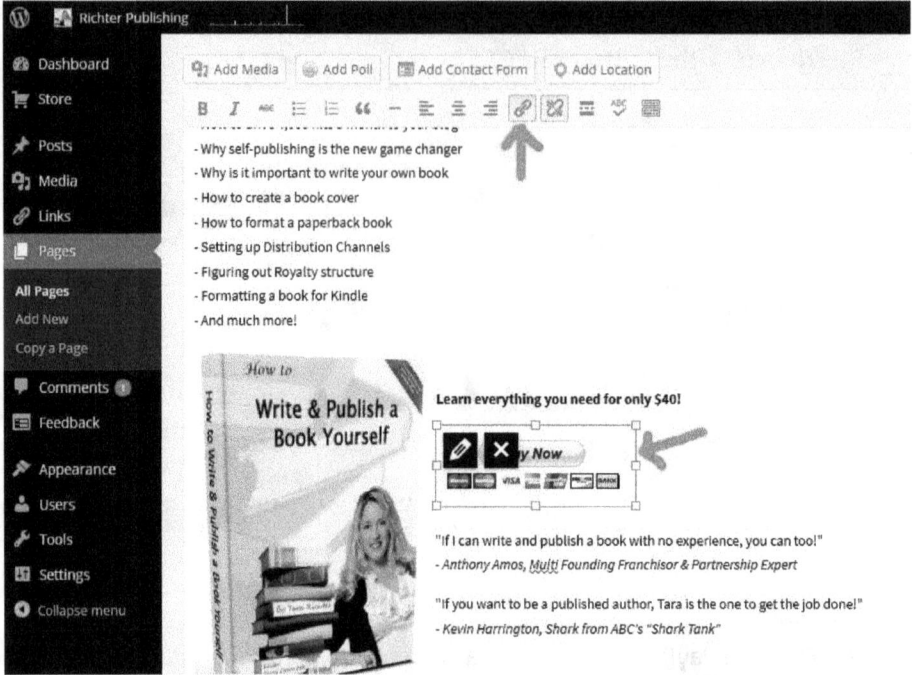

11) A box will now pop up and it will ask you to Insert/edit link information

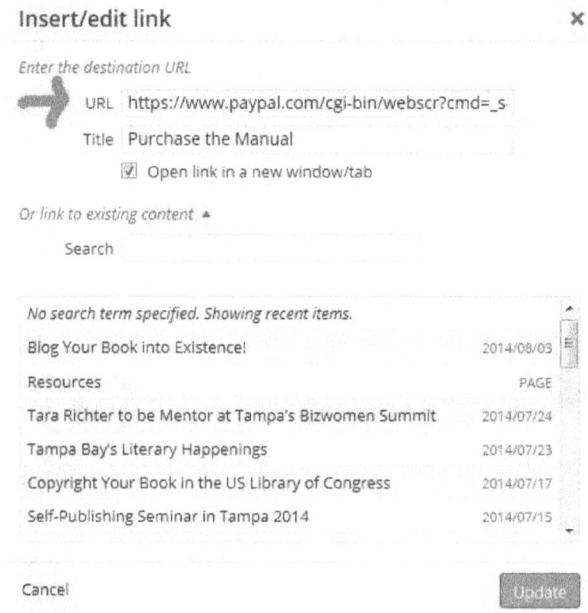

12) Now find the information you copied from your PayPal account and copy that information into the URL in this box.
13) This is the information the merchant needs to process the order.
14) When you're done click the blue UPDATE button
15) Now it will take you back to your post.
16) When you are done writing your post out, click the PUBLISH/ UPDATE button on the right hand side.

Now you need to test your button out to see if it works. If you're just updating a post will not take you to the "published" page. It will only if this is a new post. If it's not click on the VIEW PAGE button across the top. Then click your PayPal button and it will re-direct you to a PayPal page with your book purchase information!

CHAPTER 8 KEY ITEMS TO REMEMBER

1) **Be persistent**. In order to receive grand results you must keep adding content to your blog. Make sure to blast a post at least 3 -4 times a week. I like to do Mondays, Wednesdays & Fridays.

2) **Write short teasers**. When you get inspired on a certain topic for your book, you maybe end up writing 10 pages or so of content. Don't post all of that in your blog. Put a few paragraphs on each subject then at the end post a link to pre-order your book. Once the reader is engaged in the information you are providing, capturing them at that moment is crucial to get sales for your book and or services.

3) **SEO**. Make sure to utilize key words to drive traffic to your blog.

4) **Pictures**. Always use a photo and name the image appropriately. I get traffic now for people googling: *Bachelor Pad Logo*, because I posted it on a blog and named the file right.

5) **Publicize.** Hook up all your other social media so your posts are blasted out into the universe. You want them out on as many platforms as possible. Its difficult keeping up with all social media, but linking them with one click of a button saves you a lot of time!

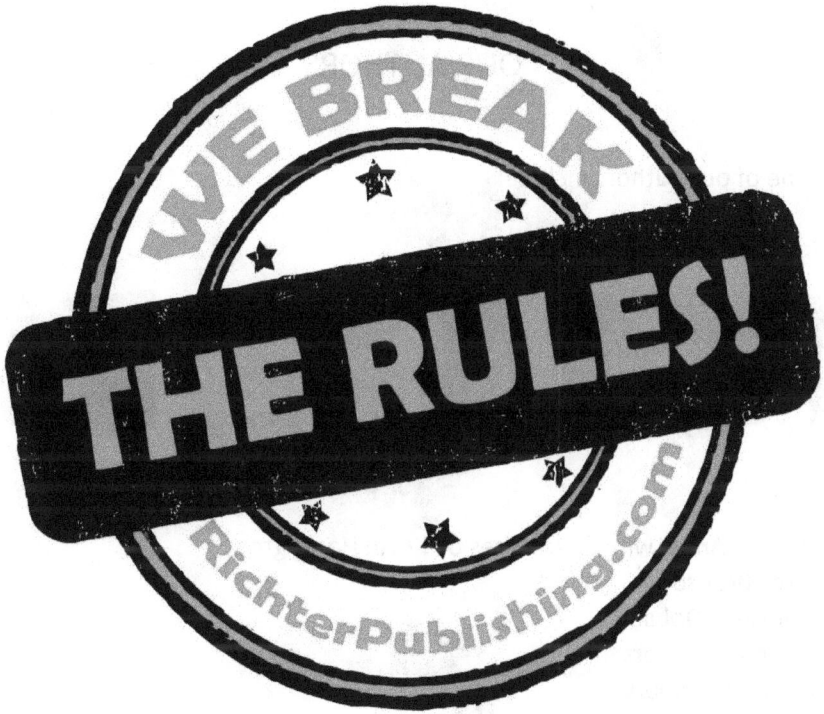

OUR AUTHORS

Some of our authors include:

Anthony Amos with Shark Bites by Kevin Harrington
Pierce Brunson
Genevieve Dobson
Meredith Rodgers
Elizabeth Bunbury
James Chittenden
Joseph Warren

To purchase books by our authors visit:
http://richterpublishing.com/featured-authors/

ABOUT THE AUTHOR

Tara Richter is the President of Richter Publishing LLC and specializes in helping business owners how to write their non-fiction story in 4 weeks & publish a book in order to become an expert in their industry. She has been featured on CNN, ABC, Daytime TV, FOX, SSN, Channel 10 News, USA TODAY & Beverly Hills Times with her "Dating Jungle Book" series.

Her degree is in Graphic Design and she worked in the copy and print industry in the Silicon Valley. She has written and published 6 of her own books in just a few short years. Tara now has published many authors in her local Tampa bay area including Anthony Amos & celebrity entrepreneur, Kevin Harrington, Shark from ABC's "Shark Tank," with their joint book, "How to Catch a Shark."

Tara was a finalist for Tampa Bay's Business Woman of the Year Awards & nominee for Tampa's Up & Coming Businesses.

Richter Publishing has streamlined the complex writing and publishing industry so anyone can become a published author in just a few weeks!

For more information on becoming an author contact us at www.richterpublishing.com

To purchase Tara's other books visit:
http://www.amazon.com/Tara-Richter/e/B00CGKD8FG/